3 Simple Steps to Better Golf

SWING FREE ™

Richard Zokol

RAINCOAST BOOKS

Vancouver

This publication contains the opinions and ideas of its author. It is not recommended by the author to perform any physical activity without professional medical approval. This publication is sold and accepted with the understanding that the author and publisher are not engaged in rendering professional medical advice. If the reader requires expert medical or other assistance in regard to their specific needs, a competent medical professional should be consulted.

The author and publisher specifically disclaim any responsibility for any injury, liability, loss or risk, personal or otherwise, which is incurred as a consequence, directly or indirectly, of the use and application of any of the contents of this book.

Raincoast Books, 8680 Cambie Street, Vancouver, B.C. V6P 6M9 (604) 323-7100

Canadian Cataloguing in Publication Data

Zokol, Richard.
Swingfree
ISBN 1-55192-225-8

1. Swing (Golf) I. Title. II. Title: Swing free
GV979.S9Z64 1999   796.352'3   C98-911045-1

Dedicated to Hal Bennett

A supportive friend who has had an inspiring impact on my perspective on life and golf.
He is a courageous man who enjoys giving rather than receiving.
I will always hold onto our pact:

"Richard, I will not be afraid of dying, if you won't be afraid of winning."

- Hal Bennett, August 28, 1997 -

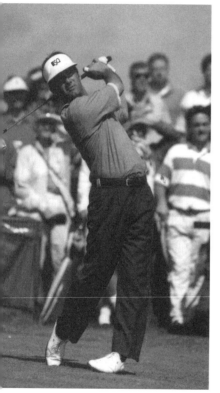

Look at Richard Zokol. There is nothing exceptional about him, not in physique, not in demeanor, not in natural golf ability. He is a family man who lives in the city where he was raised, who prefers Sundays at family barbecues to Sundays at golf tournaments. He is a business man who is making his way in the golf industry through his involvement in golf-oriented companies, including Eaglequest Golf Centers/Family Golf Centers. Yes, he is like you and he is like me: Everyman in most every respect.

Mind you, there is one significant manner in which Zokol does differ from you and me. He has played golf at the highest levels for some 20 years, on the PGA Tour, where he has won two tournaments and earned over 1.5 million (PGA Tour official) dollars. Yet the most important thing to notice here is that

Zokol, who considers himself a journeyman – no Tiger Woods or Greg Norman – elevated himself to a capable tour professional by the simple expedient of hard work, practice and dedication to his craft. Given nothing special in the way of strength, touch or psychological power, Zokol decided to get the most out of himself. An indication of his commitment was evident in how he managed to be a 'walk-on' to the Brigham Young University golf team as a freshman in 1977; that is, he was not recruited, but played his way on the team. Dick eventually captained the BYU team to the NCAA championship during his senior year in 1981. As he has told me many times, and as I have come to believe, if he can attain the highest level of the game there is no reason others cannot.

The drill you will read about here is one of the main reasons Zokol has been able to combine being a committed family and business man with making a handsome living on the PGA Tour. For the longest time Dick, a close friend whom I have known for some 20 years, searched for a way he could combine looking after his golf as well as he did his family and business life. After all, Dick was not about to leave Vancouver and move somewhere else, nor would he give up his growing interest in business. But at the same time, Dick wanted to be competitive whenever he played a tournament. How could he feel competitive when he was not playing week in week out, and when, in Vancouver during the winter months, he could not often practice?

Dick put his agile mind to work and realized that he needed to become as fit as he could for golf. The key was that he had to be fit for PGA Tour golf, not simply fit. When Dick first told me about the drills he was developing, and that they were golf-specific, I wasn't surprised. After all, this was the same fellow who had shown me a long time ago that when he sets his mind to something, he will do it – just as you can, just as anybody can.

Years ago, when I edited the Canadian golf magazine *Score* I first got to know Dick. He was just starting on the PGA Tour, having won the 1981 Canadian Amateur championship. Dick agreed to send me letters from time to time outlining his experiences on the PGA Tour. The letters were always full of insight, but it was more significant that at no time did Dick ever come up with excuses for setbacks in his own career. He took anything and everything that he went through as a learning experience.

Then along came his family – his wife Joanie and their twin boys Conor and Garrett and daughter Hayley. And then along came his interest in business. But Dick still loved golf, the playing of the game and the competing on the PGA Tour. And so he went to work finding an approach that would give him the most benefit without taking up time he just did not have.

Dick's play during the summer of 1997 demonstrated the power of his approach. He contended in both the Greater Vancouver Open and the Bell Canadian Open, tying for twelfth in the former and thirteenth in the latter. His play was marked by control and consistency, which is exactly what you will develop by doing the SwingFree™ drill.

I'm sure you don't have hours and hours a day to hit golf balls. But surely you can spare a few minutes most days, especially if you love golf as I am sure you do. I can assure you that if you spend those few minutes a day on the SwingFree drill you will find that you are almost without knowing it training your 'golf muscles'. You will be getting the most out of yourself, just as Dick has done. And I am confident that you will find that Dick is right when he says that we all can improve, that we don't need fabulous golfing genes or the gift of natural ability.

Use Dick's SwingFree drill and you will go a long way towards becoming the best golfer you can be. That's what Dick has done, and it's something you can do as well.

Lorne Rubenstein, 1998

Lorne Rubenstein is one of golf's foremost journalists. The author of:
The Natural Golf Swing, with George Knudson
Links: An Insider's Tour Through the World of Golf
Touring Prose
Rubenstein has most recently co-authored
The Swing: Mastering the Principles of the Game, Nick Price with Lorne Rubenstein, 1997.

The concept for this publication came to me in the loneliness of my Ponte Vedra Beach, Florida, hotel room during the week of the 1994 PGA Players Championship. Joanie and the kids had been on tour with me regularly in previous years, even when our twin boys, Conor and Garrett, were three months old in 1987, and after Hayley came along in 1990. But in the spring of 1994 the boys started school and the whole family stayed home in Vancouver.

In my nightly boredom, rather than watching television or reading, I decided to use the time productively. I put on my thinking cap and jotted down a few ideas on how I could possibly improve my ball-striking ability. I asked myself some questions, and I got some answers.

How can I play better? By hitting better shots with an improved swing! Sounds simple enough. How can I bring myself to swing better? By getting myself into the proper golf-swing positions when swinging the club! Would my chances of success dramatically improve if I were in a perfect position at the top of the backswing and the finished follow-through position when hitting the ball? Absolutely! How can I increase my chances of repeating my improved swing? By getting into and maintaining perfect positions at the top of the backswing and in the finished follow-through, effortlessly!

The theory is:

If you can consistently achieve the proper golf swing position at the start of your swing, at the top of your backswing and at your finished follow-through position, all the appropriate swing mechanics, along with the correct sequence throughout the swing, will be automatic.

Experimenting in my hotel room, I quickly found it was difficult to hold those positions for as much as 15 seconds, and that I really struggled to hold them for 30 seconds. When I tested my limits by holding the positions for 45 seconds, I started to perspire and my heartbeat increased dramatically. I was short of breath and I was flabbergasted. I could not understand that something that is so important to a good swing and appears easy enough is in fact so difficult to do.

The drill that I call SwingFree takes precious little time and it can be completed anywhere, at home or the office, in your hotel room or as a warm-up at the first tee. After a bit of arithmetic, I determined I'd have to put more time and energy into this drill to develop improvement in my swing consistency – in golf-specific flexibility and strength, and making my golf swing spontaneous. It's just like a Retirement Savings Plan. With regular installments of the SwingFree method, golfing assets will accrue over time, and there will be a long-lasting result of improvement – or return on your investment, if you will.

I'm a strong believer that making improvements in your golf game does not have to be a complicated procedure, and SwingFree is as basic as it comes. We choose to make golf difficult because we struggle so hard by breaking down the swing into hundreds of components.

But the game truly doesn't have to be so difficult, so complex, so intimidating. Keep it simple. That is the basis of the SwingFree method.

"Man's mind stretched to a new idea
never goes back to its original dimensions."
- Oliver Wendell Holmes -

Golf is <u>NOT</u> a Logical Game

Most sports require motion, timing, and coordination. Picture Mark McGwire hitting a baseball, Michael Chang returning a serve in tennis or Michael Jordan making a final second jump shot. Each of these actions is an 'automatic' reflex that does not require 'logical' thought since there is simply no time to plan the sequence of actions that constitute the catch or the shot. It is important to understand why golfers should not place conscious or logical thought on positions of the golf swing while in motion.

How the human brain reacts in relation to these movements, is no different for the Jordans, McGwires and Tiger Woodses of the world than it is for you and me. This automatic response is governed by the right side of the brain that tells the muscles of the body how to react and respond whatever the situation. The other side of the brain - the left side - governs all logical concepts, sequential and verbal thought. When we are completely in synch, the two hemispheres work in synergy driving us to optimal performance. When the left and right sides do not act in unison, the result is physical and mental confusion and indecision: mechanical

breakdown of the golf swing, the air ball in basketball or simply inferior shots. Typically, this problem occurs when the 'logical' brain overrides the 'automatic' reflex. When this blockage occurs, the desired swing and shot are almost impossible.

In the ideal situation, the right hemisphere is allowed to automatically compute the way to hit the ball and how hard to swing the golf club, given the distance to the green and other environmental factors. Too often the left side hampers this process by interfering with the mechanics of the golf swing (wrist position, the swing plane, etc). Some golfers may recognize this as 'forcing a shot', 'trying too hard', 'choking', or simply this logical thought triggers the intuitive sense that something is wrong.

This golf fitness program that you are reading is designed specifically to allow your right and left hemispheres to act in harmony. Its sole purpose is to condition your muscles and brain for acquiring comfort and confidence during the golf swing. The results? Better shots, and lower and more consistent scores.

Flexibility & Your Golf Swing

Flexibility is fundamental to golf. An effective swing is one in which all of your muscles interact naturally to move the club fluidly through the key swing positions. Unfortunately, desk jobs, sedentary lives and creaky joints rob most of us of the flexibility we need as golfers, and it only gets worse as we get older. You may understand the mechanics of the perfect golf swing inside and out, but if your body will not let you translate that knowledge into a smooth motion, you are fighting a losing battle. Only with flexibility – and the right kind of flexibility for golf – will you achieve the consistency needed for real improvement.

While golfers have traditionally paid little attention to physical fitness, the emphasis has been increasing steadily in recent years. PGA Tour professionals are leading the way by demonstrating the effectiveness of exercise, not only in honing their skills when they are young, but also in maintaining them as they get older.

The proof is that more and more players are staying competitive on the PGA Tour at what were considered 'advanced' ages. Flexibility is the key to longevity in the game. It's the core of every professional's exercise program.

SwingFree is not intended to compare you to PGA Tour players but to help you discover and use the same model for success, relative to your ability, as the best who play the game. By using this drill, you will maximize the time and effort you spend improving your game.

SwingFree is an exercise that is designed precisely to help golfers at all levels attain and maintain the flexibility that is necessary to make an effective golf-swing. The drill has two important aspects:

- It increases your golf strength and flexibility to allow you to swing properly in a fluid motion.

- It educates your mind and body, through repetition, to find and recognize the fundamentally correct positions of:

1. The Starting Position

2. The Completed Backswing Position

3. The Finished Follow-through Position

Once you get on the golf course, the moment of truth, your body will have the flexibility and familiarity with the crucial elements of the swing to repeat these movements naturally.

SwingFree is simple to do, no matter how busy and stressful your life off the golf course may be. Many golfers spend a lot of time at a desk and find it difficult to work out regularly. But SwingFree is designed to be done at home, in the office, or at the golf course before, during or after a round of golf.

Some great golfers are enthusiastic about this drill, but my favorite endorsement comes from a much tougher critic – my father, a member of the Marine Drive Golf Club in Vancouver. Planted firmly for many years as an 18-handicap, Dad agreed to try out this drill in the spring of 1994, when he was 72 years old. While doing the drill regularly for two weeks he made steady improvement; he soon found that his game stabilized and shot 79. After another week he saw further improvement and shot a 77. His confidence climbed. Another two weeks passed and he almost hit that elusive milestone termed 'shooting your age', he was two strokes short with a 74. His handicap dropped to a 10 and his friends noticed the improvement and paid attention to what he was doing. My father sustained a 10 handicap for two years from that point and has remained faithful to his commitment to the drill.

There is nothing magical about that rapid improvement. You can expect the same dramatic results, if your commitment is strong and you follow the guidelines. The SwingFree drill consists of a series of exercises that take a total of 10 to 20 minutes to complete. It takes a little effort but mostly discipline to follow this method through to success. If you are committed to improving your golf game, I recommend doing the SwingFree drill five days a week, every week. The discipline is making this drill a part of your daily routine. As your scores drop, I think you'll agree it is time well invested.

"We are not limited by our old age;
we are liberated by it."
- Stu Mittleman -

Any stretching and exercise program could do your golf game some good. However, the SwingFree method is different; it programs your body and mind specifically for the golf swing. Repetition of this drill trains your body and mind to apply your improved golf swing on the course and helps you perform efficiently. You become aware of what you 'should be doing' when you swing, rather than having your mind cluttered with those negative thoughts of what you 'shouldn't be doing'. You simply develop an effective swing motion. In fact, the drill is as much a matter of bringing mind and body into harmony as it is about toning and stretching your golf muscles.

One thing to keep in mind: every individual's level of flexibility is different. You must be responsible and aware of your own physical limitations at the outset. Consult your doctor for your specific needs before doing any physical program. To begin with, stretch only to a position that you can maintain without harm. If you feel pain that causes you too much discomfort or pain that could cause damage, you should stop immediately.

As the drill becomes part of your routine, your flexibility will improve to make it easier to reach and hold the correct positions. Before we start, understanding the Code for Effortless Power will assist you in realizing the significant value of SwingFree.

"We are, or become, those things we repeatedly do. Therefore, excellence can become not just an event but a habit."

- Albert Einstein -

The Code for Effortless Power

The Law of Least Resistance: "Perform less and achieve more"

Even fit individuals often find that flexibility gets short shrift in their normal exercise regime. In North America and Europe, we tend to put more emphasis these days on cardiovascular fitness, strength and muscle tone. But other cultures have long understood the importance of stretching, especially as we get older.

The ancient Chinese system of calisthenics called tai chi uses a series of repeated motions and held positions to promote strength and flexibility for the body and mind. Tai chi is said to enhance a Zen-like serenity. Nothing contributes to a golfer's inner calm like having confidence in his or her ability to strike the ball consistently well. All golfers would improve their levels of play and tap into intuitive ability if they viewed golf as martial arts – powerful, graceful movement in total balance rather than as a geometrical equation of mechanics that one must figure out with the logical mind. Like tai chi, SwingFree is a system with some basic principles. I will explain these in this chapter.

Effortless Power is the ability to do an act at the highest level, in precise and simple form, accompanied by no wasted movement at all.

All athletes at the highest level of competition achieve Effortless Power to some degree. A player who remains among the best of the best over an extended period takes Effortless Power to the highest grade. The finest example of Effortless Power on the PGA Tour today is Tiger Woods. We have only seen Tiger in the short term, but what a short term it has been. In his rookie year he had five victories in 16 starts on the PGA Tour, including the record breaking score (-18) at the Masters that destroyed the field, and he made $2,066,833 in his first full year of official PGA Tour earnings. He seems to have what it takes to succeed over the long term.

Tiger is taking Effortless Power to a new level and is raising the bar for everyone else. At this point Tiger has two Distinct Competitive Advantages over his competition and they are:

1. Achieving a higher physical ability, with less effort.

2. His apparent and unique ability of not being plagued by self-doubt.

Tiger possesses correct swing fundamentals together with remarkable flexibility in total balance. This generates significant club head speed and controlled power. The combination of these details is essential for Effortless Power. The principal element that Tiger possesses is his mental state in the form of his belief in his ability. It is Tiger's strong conviction and belief in his ability that allows his actions to follow through to complete his desired goal.

Not since the arrival of Jack Nicklaus on the PGA Tour has there been such a gap of ability between one player and the others. Nicklaus brought a superior physical golf game when he showed up as a rookie on the PGA Tour. Still, a remarkable physical ability is not enough. Jack's greatest asset has always been controlling his mind first and foremost.

Greg Norman definitely possesses the power, but he often comes up short in his ability to consistently contain and control his swing, which means inevitably containing and controlling his thoughts. Norman has had some great achievements, but if he is to fulfill his potential in the world of golf, it is essential that he tap into the ability to first control his thoughts. Golf can be simple . . . if it is first played with the mind, then with the body.

Tiger's martial art-like golf ability allows him to accomplish a higher rate of power and control, with less energy, more consistently than the current PGA Tour standard. The mechanics of Tiger's swing are extremely sound, as are those of most PGA Tour professionals. However, the source that enables him to produce his physical power and set up a distinct competitive advantage is his remarkable flexibility. The leverage generated by his golf specific flexibility, accompanied with his complete swing mechanics, gives him the edge.

When amateur golfers witness world class professional golfers, they marvel at their awesome power and ability to control the flight of the golf ball at will. What is puzzling to the amateur is the ease and high precision with which these professionals repeat each shot.

Being Calm

Being *Calm*, or quieting the logical mind, is essential for good golf. *Calming* the logical mind allows our natural 'intuitive' ability to surface. This, in turn, empowers the portion of our mind that is *appropriate* for understanding and solving the task at hand: playing *golf*.

I am sure that, like all golfers, you have experienced the frustrations that come with playing the game. In order to overcome these continual mistakes, we must begin to understand that a hyperactive logical mind does not serve golfers well; in fact, it is detrimental to playing golf well.

Feelings of being anxious, fearful, upset or angry are rooted in the hyperactive logical mind. In order to play effective golf, one must continually strive to *calm* the logical mind.

You must not force your efforts with a golf swing or a putt; this is a harmful characteristic that your logical mind directs. Once the basic fundamentals are in place the golf motion requires rhythm and feel, which is enhanced when the mind is *calm*.

Being Relaxed

The state of being *relaxed* is powerful. Being *calm* is to the mind as *relaxing* is to the body. *Relaxing* allows freedom of movement, for greater speed of motion, in balance. Effortless Power cannot be accomplished without the state of *relaxation*.

A known fact of *relaxation*, as it pertains to golf, is the effect it has on enhancing our sense of feel. When all golfers perform to their highest abilities, they enter states of *relaxation*.

One of Fred Couples' greatest attributes is his ability to *relax* on the golf course during competition. Given his talent, Fred knows there are not too many golf shots that he cannot make, which is the basis for his confidence. Fred's natural ability to *relax* gives him an added edge against his competitors. When a situation becomes intense, Fred's natural *relaxed* state maintains his competitive advantage. Fred has always found a deep comfort on the golf course in competition.

As Couples' close friend, CBS sportscaster Jim Nantz, puts it, *"Fred's swing mirrors his personality, which is totally relaxed and effortless."*

Centering

Centering is regulating and placing your awareness on your center of gravity. Centering is essential to all movement and motion. When we walk, we control our center of gravity automatically, shifting our weight from one foot to the other in a fluid motion. The golf swing is no different.

Centering is essential for all athletic movement. The graceful power of an Olympic figure skater is a great example of athletic centering in motion. PGA touring pro Steve Elkington's graceful and powerful golf swing is another. Elkington and other top players develop and control their balance by controlling their center of gravity. If your *center of gravity* is erratic while you swing the golf club, so will your golf shots be erratic.

Masters of the martial arts teach their students: "Move from your center and your body will follow." Put in lay terms for golf, this means, if you are centered (*in balance*) at the Starting Position, the Completed Backswing Position and at the Finished Follow-through Position, the proper motion, mechanics and sequence will result.

Make a goal out of discovering and mastering your *center* in these three fundamental positions. All golfers are capable of breakthroughs with their golf game, if they choose to approach the game much like martial arts. Free yourself from your old ways of thinking and you will liberate yourself to a new way of swinging.

Following the basic fundamentals of the SwingFree method, that is what you will achieve. Once you begin to move from your *center* of your Starting Position, to the center of your Completed Backswing Position, then firing to the *center* of your Finished Follow-through Position, you will be well on your way to awakening the productive golf swing that you know you are capable of repeating.

Unity

Golf instructors who teach students to move the arms, shoulders, hips and so on independently of each other, teach a method difficult for your mind to comprehend and therefore repeat. If you find yourself thinking and swinging the way I have just described, the all too familiar result – 'fighting yourself' with your swing – continues the typical frustration cycle.

The term *unity* is intended to convey the importance of the parts of your body working together. It is important to appreciate that all the movements of the golf swing follow the direction of the *center*.

Contrary to what many people believe, nobody is given the gift of being an excellent golfer. When you witness PGA Tour or other world class players hitting golf balls, seemingly with Effortless Power, you should recognize that getting into that state has for them been anything but 'effortless'. I can assure you that they have invested a great deal of time and effort in developing their talents.

All who excel in any form of athletics or movement follow the code. Athletes lock on to the feedback they get when they train for their sport. Their acute awareness of their bodies, constantly monitoring their own progress, leads them to focus on whatever helps them to improve.

The Code for Effortless Power is essential for high performance at all levels. As with the martial arts, so it is with the game of golf: the route to success is always a journey, never a destination.

How To Apply Effortless Power To Your Golf Game

Pledge and follow through to achieving the simple fundamentals of the SwingFree™ drill. When performing the drill and breathing in a rhythmic pattern, settle your thoughts on:

Being Calm
(calming your thoughts)

Being Relaxed
(relaxing your body in the required positions)

Centering
(control your center of gravity while in the fundamental positions and swing motion)

Unity
(move from your center and all body movement will be automatic)

"If we all did the things we were capable of doing, we would literally astound ourselves."

- Thomas A. Edison -

SwingFree the Drill

It's a Matter of 3 Simple Steps

Step #1: The Starting Position

It is important to always use an actual golf club. This is what you will be using when you play – with its characteristic heft and feel – so it should be what you use when you are training. To start, adopt your usual stance before swinging. Be aware of the following fundamentals:

1. Keep your knees bent and directly over the balls of your feet (not over your heels or toes);

2. Bend at the waist, with your back flat and spine straight (this creates your spine angle);

3. Set your feet approximately shoulder width apart.

Become aware of your center of gravity (center point) and make it a mental reference point. When you find and feel this center point, you have just 'centered'

in the Starting Position. The objective is to control your starting position center point. Through repetition of this drill you will learn to center automatically in this position. Centering in the starting position of every swing is the intended result of our practices. When you spend time in this position, learning and developing control of your center, breathe deeply and rhythmically – and relax. Rhythmic breathing patterns and relaxation will enhance your ability to control your center.

As I mentioned in chapter one, you can do the SwingFree drill almost anytime, anywhere. I recommend practicing the drill first thing in the morning after warming up in a hot shower. This loosens your muscles and directs the first actions of the day to improving your golf swing.

Notice the spine angle

1. Shoulder width stance
2. Weight distribution
   50% left foot
   50% right foot

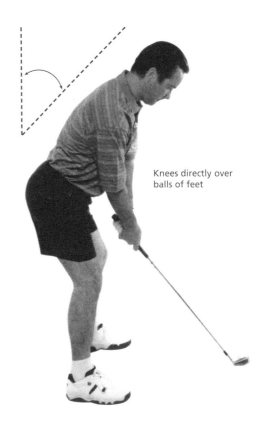

Knees directly over balls of feet

Step #2: The Completed Backswing Position

The Completed Backswing Position is the complete extended position of the backswing when you have 75 percent of your weight over the instep and ball of your right foot (as a right-handed golfer). (Reverse the instructions in this section if you are left handed.) Your Spine Angle—straight spine or flat back, bent from the waist—should be unchanged from Step #1. Your torso should have rotated entirely so that your back is squarely facing to your target. Your right knee should be slightly bent and directly over the ball of your right foot. Your left shoulder should be touching or directly under your chin.

While in this position extend your hands as high as you can, and now consider your golf club. The shaft should be pointing toward your target. Don't worry whether your shaft is at parallel, beyond, or short of being parallel to the ground. Remember, keep your back square to your target. Hold the position and breathe deeply in a rhythmic pattern for 20 seconds. Keep your eye on a clock, or put your watch on a desktop where you can see it.

Once again as in Step #1, become aware of your center of gravity (center point) in this position and make it a mental reference point. When you find this center point, you are learning to be centered in the Completed Backswing Position. **The objective is to control your completed backswing center point.** Your goal should be to learn through repetition of this drill to automatically center in this position. When you spend time in this position, you learn and develop control of your center. Again, breathe deeply and rhythmically, and *relax*.

After 20 seconds, come out of the stretch and relax. Do two more repetitions when you feel ready. Three repetitions is a complete set. Already, you will likely have spent more time assuming and holding the proper backswing position than you would in many rounds of golf.

You are now achieving the feeling of being in the correct, fundamental position — a marvelous sensation. This is the beginning of what is called neuromuscular memory. In order to build that sensation deep into your central nervous system, you need to do this on a regular basis and make it habitual. This will lead to major improvement at a personal level.

1. Back square to target
2. Spine angle has not changed from step #1

Weight transfer
to right foot
25% left foot
75% right foot

Right knee
remains over ball
of right foot

25

Step #3: The Finished Follow-through Position

After your final repetition of the Completed Backswing Position, instead of stopping to relax, swing the club through to the Finished Follow-through Position. **Your weight should transfer from the ball of the right foot (in Step #2) to the ball of the left foot. Be sure not to shift weight to the toes or the heel of the left foot.** (Again, reverse these instructions if you are left handed.) Maintain the same Spine Angle as in Step #1 and Step #2. Most people will experience some restriction, tightness or even pain through holding the Spine Angle in this position. This is an indication that attention to stretching and centering in this area is most important.

You should now have 90 percent of your weight on the ball of your left foot, with your torso and hips facing square to the target. Once again, hold this position and breathe deeply in a rhythmic pattern for 20 seconds.

As in Step #1 and Step #2, become aware of your center of gravity in this position and make it a mental reference point. When you find this center point, you are learning to be centered in the Finished Follow-through Position. **The objective is to control your follow-through center point.**

After 20 seconds come out of the stretch and relax. Do two more repetitions of the same stretch when you feel ready to do so. When you have completed three repetitions, you will have finished a full rotation of the SwingFree drill. (No need to practice Step #4: the position when you raise your hand up to shield your eyes from the sun to watch the ball drop exactly where you wanted it to go).

As a PGA Tour professional, I have worked up to holding and centering in my positions for one full minute in Step #2 and Step #3 for each repetition. Still, every morning when I start my drill routine the tightness and restriction is ever-present and uncomfortable, although now I can loosen up my swing at a fast rate. Completing a full cycle of this drill equals a premium golf workout that builds structure into your golf swing for all levels.

Tightening of back muscles on the golf course is common to all golfers, especially late in the round. Spending a few moments doing this drill on the back nine, when you feel your back tighten up, will allow you to finish as strongly as you felt when you started the round.

1. Spine angle has not changed from step #1 and step #2
2. Weight transferred to ball of left foot

Weight transferred to left side

1. Front of torso square to target
2. hands extended high

"We first make our habits,
and then our habits
make us."

- John Dryden -

The Essence of the Drill

Consider a little scenario, unlikely though it may be. A golfer plays 18 holes every day and hits 100 practice balls as well. Assume also that he makes a perfect swing each and every time, momentarily attaining Steps #2 and Step #3 of our drill with each swing. Not even the top PGA Tour professionals achieve this consistency. But even if we assume this is the case, our super-golfer would only realize the optimum positions of the SwingFree drill for a fraction of a second with each swing.

Let's assume, generously, that, for every perfect swing, the swing position represented in Step #2 takes ¼ of a second. In addition, the swing position represented in Step #3 takes ¼ of a second. That's a total of ½ a second. That's a total of ½ a second per golf swing spent in the two critical positions. Also, let's assume the golfer shoots 90 each round. Let's run through the arithmetic. Subtract, say 36 putts per 18 holes, which leaves 54 perfect full swings, along with those 100 perfect swings on the practice tee. That's 154 multiplied by ½ a second for a total of 77 seconds per day.

In my opinion, spending 77 seconds a day is nowhere near enough time for your mind and body to make intricate adjustments of the key golf positions second nature. Nor is it enough time for your mind and body to start working together effortlessly to repeat the golf swing you want.

Now, you and I are not playing 18 holes a day, no matter how much we'd love to. Most of us do not have enough time and discipline to hit 100 balls on the practice tee before every round, not by a long shot.

Indeed, the truth is that if you are an average golfer you probably rarely attain the correct positions outlined in this scenario, let alone reach them with predictable consistency. The results, though, are all too easy to project: uncertainty of how to swing, muscle atrophy, muscle weakness, lack of flexibility, and disappointing shot making.

Your game stands to improve dramatically if you do the SwingFree drill five days a week. The improvement will persist as long as you continue this method, simply because the specific positions most important to producing a good golf swing will become encoded in your mind and every muscle, cartilage and tendon. New habits that translate into a better golf swing will replace the old bad habits that were ingrained. The old tightness around the shoulders, the lower back and the knees will ease. Just as crucial, that unnerving feeling of not truly knowing the feeling of the proper swing positions will give way to a new-found sense of certainty. More and more often, you will slip into the groove. It's a great feeling.

SwingFree sounds simple – and is simple! Albeit, many golfers will discover that 20-second repetitions in Step #2 and Step #3 will be too much to complete comfortably at the start. If so, begin by trying 10 seconds for each stretch, increasing the duration to 15 seconds after one week, and up to the full 20 seconds in the third.

After you gain comfort and confidence in this drill, work up to holding these proper positions for extended time in reach of your personal ability, up to one minute in each position. The objective is the continual improvement of golf specific strength and flexibility.

As I have suggested and if you are able to stretch, strengthen and hold Step

#2 and Step #3 for one minute per repetition, repeat the entire cycle three times. That means three minutes or 180 seconds in each of Step #2 and Step #3. At that rate, you should spend 360 seconds daily in the two critical swing positions, far more than the daily quota of 77 seconds our super-golfer managed or a 467 percent increase. If we were to look at the average golfer's time spent in Step #2 and Step #3, the percentage of improvement would be more on the order of over 1,000 percent. Draw your own conclusion about the benefits of stretching into the crucial positions for nearly five times longer every day than even our best-case scenario offered.

You could benefit still more, depending on your level of commitment. A mere 10-20 minutes a day invested in the SwingFree method puts you well on your way to ingraining the fundamental elements of golf.

What you will be purchasing with this daily installment plan is more pleasure for your golfing future. Golf is important to so many of us because it marries the capacity of the body with the clarity of the mind like no other game. There is no reason for that connection to weaken as we get older. Again, I think of my 78-year-young father. He enjoys his golf more than ever because his game has improved so markedly. It's that potential for improvement that lies at the heart of our pastime's remarkable popularity.

*"The beginning of a habit is like an invisible thread,
but every time we repeat the act we strengthen the strand,
add to it another filament, until it becomes a great cable
and binds us irrevocably, thought and act."*

- Orison Swett Marden -

One important objective of this game is to achieve a state of relaxed concentration that yields you the optimum frame of mind before every swing of the golf club. But unless you possess the physical strength, flexibility and the neuromuscular memory to convert that concentration into the controlled explosion of an effective swing, the aesthetics of golf can quickly deteriorate into frustration. The SwingFree drill is designed for people with today's demands, with real time constraints and a genuine desire to improve.

SwingFree is the golf swing made simple. It is based on the understanding that every swing of every round of golf is built on three precise positions. Making the SwingFree drill part of your daily routine is about infusing those key positions in your game as never before. It's that simple. In the time it took you to read this book, you can complete a full cycle of the SwingFree drill.

Let's get started.

"It is not enough to have
a good mind; the main
thing is to use it well"

- Rene Descartes -

My biggest fans are my parents. I will be forever indebted to them for their non-stop encouragement and enthusiasm. Without them I might never have been introduced to this great game.

While growing up in Vancouver, B.C., my Dad took me to Marine Drive Golf Club to caddy for him when I was 10-years old. As soon as we were out of sight of the clubhouse, he'd throw out a ball for me to whack at with an old five-iron he had cut down. Two years later, my parents got me a junior membership. As we lived only three houses from the corner of the entrance to the club, I earned pocket money as a regular weekend caddy for an extraordinary man, the late L.L.G. Bentley. I feel very fortunate my parents were able to support me financially as well as emotionally to be a walk-on at Brigham Young University. They allowed me to further my golf development when I wasn't skillful enough to earn a scholarship.

I can't say enough about the support of my wife. Joanie has been my strength through good times and bad. The only other people who can appreciate the adversity it takes to overcome to play the PGA Tour are the pros themselves. Joanie's always been there for me; she had faith even when I questioned it. I've always turned to her basic common sense as a resource and to her objective viewpoint. She has the kind of inside knowledge that's only recognized by players or their wives. My children Conor, Garrett and Hayley keep my life journey in the proper perspective. They love me because I am their Dad, regardless of how I play golf. They are a source of my inspiration.

Karl Tucker, Alvie Thompson and Clay Edwards are golf experts who have most profoundly impacted me as a golfer and a person. Tucker, the Brigham Young University golf coach, is like a father to all of us who played for him. He contributed more to his players than he got credit for, developing and creating a successful environment and a will to win both on and off the golf course. Playing for Tucker and being a part of the BYU golf team that won the 1981 NCAA Championship is truly one of the greatest moments in my golfing career. Thompson, the head pro at Marine Drive when I was a young junior, initially guided me in the right direction. He is someone very close to my heart, someone I admire immensely. I am grateful to Moe Norman for introducing me in 1983 to Edwards, who's a most insightful golf instructor. He has been largely responsible for designing and developing my golfing knowledge and philosophy. He opened my eyes as to how I play the game today. Importantly, he taught me to independently analyze my own swing. I don't panic in seeking a special instructor when the mechanics of my swing sputter.

In the early 1970s I met Russ Jordan, who became my best friend. Russ and I learned to play junior golf competition at Marine Drive and we were a strong threat on the Magee High School golf team. Russ and I share a special friendship, none more exciting than when he caddied for me while I was in contention in the final round in the 1992 U.S. Open at Pebble Beach.

I've enjoyed wonderful assistance in creating this publication, in fact throughout my career on and off the course. I'm grateful to Family Golf Centers for giving me the opportunity to develop the business component in my life and to all of those people who have encouraged me along the way.

With apologies to anyone I might have overlooked.
I'm especially grateful to:

Raincoast Books
Perry Goldsmith, Contemporary Communications/NSB
Bill Stobbe
B/W Golf Images – Robert Walker
David Fergusson
Lorne Rubenstein
Arv Olson
SCORE Magazine, Bob Weeks, Kim Locke, Alan Coulson
Jackson Sayers Fitness
Photos – Darryl Harapiak. Lionel Trudel
Mike O'Donnell
Dr. Ralph Strother

Stephen Geddes; Gordon Brooks; Lyall Knott; Deborah Zokol; Peter Radiuk;
Stephen Neal; John Robb; Tim Tait; Rob Hazeldine; Don Wallace; Mike Francis;
Bob Lavelle; Chan Buckland; Blake Corosky; Kevin Craib; John Durrant;
Bob & Jean Garnett; Robert Safrata; Robert Mackwood; Jason Monteleone;
Steve Sidwell; Shelly Woolner; Elmer Cheng; Keith Sanden; Beau Faust;
Ted Naff; Michael Downes; Brad Pelletier; Scott Kuester.

Your SwingFree™ Practice Diary

Date & Time	Time Spent in Position #1 (Seconds)	Time Spent in Position #2 (Seconds)	Time spent in Position #3 (Seconds)	Recent Scores	Handicap	Comments

Date & Time	Time Spent in Position #1 (*Seconds*)	Time Spent in Position #2 (*Seconds*)	Time spent in Position #3 (*Seconds*)	Recent Scores	Handicap	Comments

Date & Time	Time Spent in Position #1 (*Seconds*)	Time Spent in Position #2 (*Seconds*)	Time spent in Position #3 (*Seconds*)	Recent Scores	Handicap	Comments

Date & Time	Time Spent in Position #1 (Seconds)	Time Spent in Position #2 (Seconds)	Time spent in Position #3 (Seconds)	Recent Scores	Handicap	Comments

Date & Time	Time Spent in Position #1 (*Seconds*)	Time Spent in Position #2 (*Seconds*)	Time spent in Position #3 (*Seconds*)	Recent Scores	Handicap	Comments

Date & Time	Time Spent in Position #1 (Seconds)	Time Spent in Position #2 (Seconds)	Time spent in Position #3 (Seconds)	Recent Scores	Handicap	Comments

Date & Time	Time Spent in Position #1 (Seconds)	Time Spent in Position #2 (Seconds)	Time spent in Position #3 (Seconds)	Recent Scores	Handicap	Comments

Date & Time	Time Spent in Position #1 (*Seconds*)	Time Spent in Position #2 (*Seconds*)	Time spent in Position #3 (*Seconds*)	Recent Scores	Handicap	Comments

Date & Time	Time Spent in Position #1 (*Seconds*)	Time Spent in Position #2 (*Seconds*)	Time spent in Position #3 (*Seconds*)	Recent Scores	Handicap	Comments

Date & Time	Time Spent in Position #1 (*Seconds*)	Time Spent in Position #2 (*Seconds*)	Time spent in Position #3 (*Seconds*)	Recent Scores	Handicap	Comments